Frida Kahlo

Copyright © 2017 by Quelle Histoire / quellehistoire.com
Published by Roaring Brook Press
Roaring Brook Press is a division of Holtzbrinck Publishing Holdings Limited Partnership
175 Fifth Avenue, New York, NY 10010
mackids.com
All rights reserved

Library of Congress Control Number: 2018936548
ISBN 978-1-250-16875-7

Our books may be purchased in bulk for promotional, educational, or business use. Please contact your
local bookseller or the Macmillan Corporate and Premium Sales Department at (800) 221-7945 ext. 5442
or by e-mail at MacmillanSpecialMarkets@macmillan.com.

First published in France in 2017 by Quelle Histoire, Paris
First U.S. edition, 2018

Text: Clémentine V. Baron
Translation: Catherine Nolan
Illustrations: Bruno Wennagel, Mathieu Ferret, Aurélie Verdon, Guillaume Biasse, Mathilde Tuffin,
Nuno Alves Rodrigues

Printed in China by RR Donnelley Asia Printing Solutions Ltd., Dongguan City, Guangdong Province
10 9 8 7 6 5 4 3 2 1

Frida Kahlo

Roaring Brook Press
New York

The Blue House

Frida Kahlo was a world-famous painter from Mexico. She was born Magdalena Frida Carmen Kahlo y Calderón in 1907. She had three sisters. One of them, Cristina, was Frida's best friend for her entire life. The girls grew up in a pretty blue house that their father built in a neighborhood of Mexico City.

———

1907

Polio

When she was six years old, Frida felt pains in her right leg. Doctors discovered that she had polio, a disease that would keep her leg from growing properly.

Frida tried to hide her leg under wide pants, long skirts, and tall socks. But bullies at school taunted her. They nicknamed her "Peg-Leg Frida."

Luckily, Frida's family showered her with love. Her father was a photographer, and he taught Frida all about taking pictures. She learned to think like an artist at an early age!

——

1913

The Accident

One September day in 1925, Frida was riding a bus home from school. The bus was hit by a streetcar, and Frida was badly hurt.

She spent weeks in the hospital, then months in bed at home. While she was recovering, Frida began to paint. Most of the paintings were of herself. She had a mirror hung on her ceiling so she could see her own face.

———

1925

The Message of Pain

Frida used bold, cheerful colors in her paintings. But her pictures were not happy ones. Frida was hurting a lot from her accident, and she showed it by painting herself with tears, blood, and broken bones. "My painting contains in it the message of pain," she said.

Painting helped Frida find relief from her suffering. Finally, she began to feel joy again.

———

1925

The Dove and the Elephant

Frida worked up the courage to show a well-known Mexican artist named Diego Rivera some of her paintings. Diego was impressed. He told Frida to keep painting and began visiting her to see her work. Soon, the two artists fell in love.

Frida was a tiny woman. Diego was a big man. When Frida told her parents that she was going to marry him, they declared, "It's the wedding of a dove and an elephant!"

———

1925–1929

Far From Home

Frida and Diego got married in 1929. The next year, Diego was invited to paint some outdoor paintings, called *frescoes*, in the United States.

Frida and Diego moved to San Francisco, then to Detroit, and at last to New York City.

Diego liked America, but Frida missed Mexico. She started painting lush pictures of her country. She was very glad when the time came to go back.

———

1929–1933

Success

Back in Mexico, Frida welcomed important people into her home. One of them was Leon Trotsky, a Russian politician. Another was André Breton, a French writer.

André called Frida's paintings "surrealist." Surrealist art mixed together dreams and ordinary life. Frida did not care much for the name. "I never knew I was a surrealist until André Breton came to Mexico and told me I was," she said. "I myself still don't know what I am."

André helped set up an exhibition for Frida in New York. She sold more than half of her paintings! Frida was becoming a big success.

1933–1938

Frida and the Fridos

Frida began teaching at the Ministry of Education in Mexico City. She called her students the "Fridos." She took them through the city streets and around the countryside so they could capture Mexico's beauty and spirit.

Frida loved her work, but her health was failing. Soon, she couldn't walk. So Frida invited the "Fridos" to her home. They painted in her lovely garden.

1943

Final Exhibition

In 1953, an exhibition honoring Frida's work was put together in Mexico. Frida wanted to go, but how? By now, she was very ill and weak. She had undergone several serious operations, and she was stuck in bed most of the time.

Then Frida got an idea. She would go to the exhibition . . . in bed! She dressed up in fancy clothes and decorated her bed, too. It was a clever way to enjoy the celebration.

1953

"Viva la Vida"

Frida painted her last piece of art in 1954. It showed juicy watermelons with *Viva la Vida* painted on one in bright-red letters. The words mean *Long live life*. Even though she spent much of her life in pain, Frida was determined to enjoy it, right until the end.

Frida died on July 13, 1954, but her fame kept on growing. Today, people everywhere know and admire her work. She is called one of the most important artists of her time.

———

1954

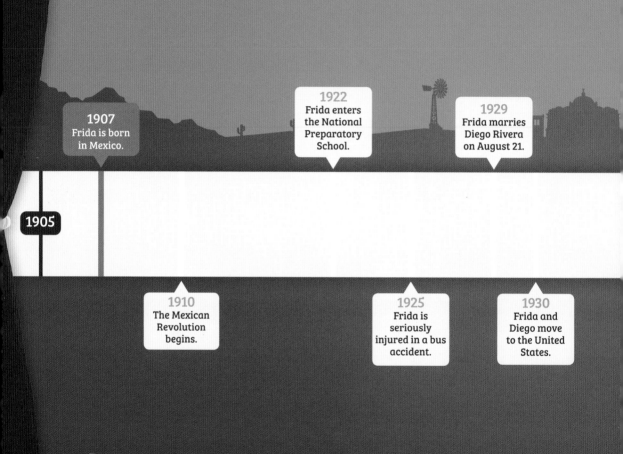

1905

1907
Frida is born in Mexico.

1910
The Mexican Revolution begins.

1922
Frida enters the National Preparatory School.

1925
Frida is seriously injured in a bus accident.

1929
Frida marries Diego Rivera on August 21.

1930
Frida and Diego move to the United States.

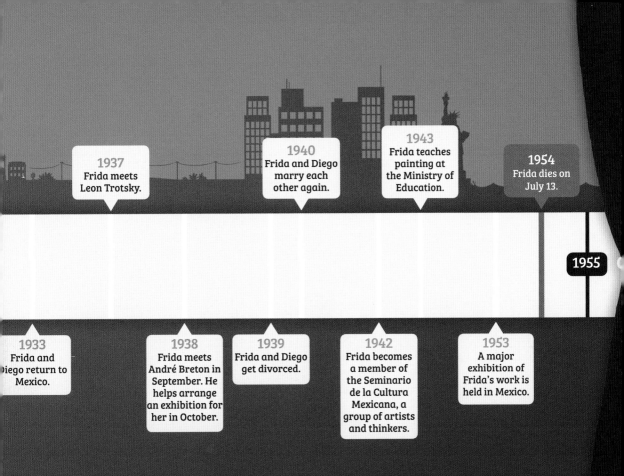

1937
Frida meets
Leon Trotsky.

1940
Frida and Diego
marry each
other again.

1943
Frida teaches
painting at
the Ministry of
Education.

1954
Frida dies on
July 13.

1955

1933
Frida and
Diego return to
Mexico.

1938
Frida meets
André Breton in
September. He
helps arrange
an exhibition for
her in October.

1939
Frida and Diego
get divorced.

1942
Frida becomes
a member of
the Seminario
de la Cultura
Mexicana, a
group of artists
and thinkers.

1953
A major
exhibition of
Frida's work is
held in Mexico.

Frida Kahlo's Journey

MAP KEY

 The Blue House,
Mexico City, Mexico

Frida was born in this house and died here at age forty-seven. Her father built the house in 1904. Today, it is a museum.

 San Francisco,
California

Frida and Diego moved to this U.S. city in November 1930.

 Detroit,
Michigan

Diego painted a large fresco here.

 San Ángel,
Mexico City, Mexico

Frida and Diego lived in this neighborhood in Mexico City after they returned from the United States.

 New York,
New York

Frida lived in New York for a few months with Diego in 1933. She returned in 1938 for an exhibition of her work.

 Paris,
France

In 1939, Frida traveled to Paris for an exhibition about Mexico.

People to Know

Diego Rivera
(1886–1957)

This Mexican painter was Frida's great love. They married, divorced, and married again!

André Breton
(1896–1966)

André led the surrealist art movement. He was deeply impressed with Frida's paintings.

Leon Trotsky
(1879–1940)
This Russian politician had to leave his country because of his beliefs. In 1936 he moved to Mexico, where he met Frida.

Lola Álvarez Bravo
(1903–1993)
Lola was a Mexican photographer, known for her strange and fantastic images. She took several portraits of Frida. Lola arranged Frida's big exhibition in Mexico in 1953.

....

Fifty-five of Frida's 143 paintings were self-portraits. She painted herself with traditional dresses and hairstyles but also with a slight mustache and thick eyebrows that met in the middle of her forehead.

....

In her lifetime, Frida had more than thirty operations because of her bus accident.

....

Frida planned to go to medical school before she became an artist.

....

Frida was born in 1907, but she told people she was born in 1910. She wanted her birthday to match the start of the Mexican Revolution.

Available Now

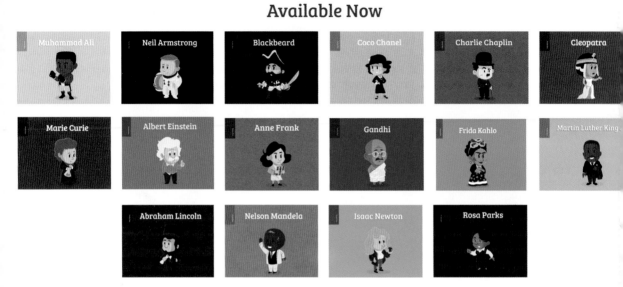

Coming Soon